THE SHARMANSCOPES IV

2023 EDITION

INTRODUCTION

Mike Sharman once again returns with this, the fourth instalment of "The Sharmanscopes". Written for you to giggle, groan, chuckle and sigh, perhaps they may very well hint at what a typical week has in store for you!

Having previously written and published "The Sharmanscopes 2013", "The Sharmanscopes 2014" and "The Sharmanscopes 2020 - A Week In Lockdown", Mike continues to entertain with this new collection of gigglers and groaners, produced ten years after his first book was put on sale.

Seven days, twelve star signs and "amazing" predictions on your daily life!

All delivered in Mike's trademark tongue-in-cheek style, please enjoy this release from the stresses of the day-to-day world and enter the world of the Sharmanscopes.

Mike originally wrote and performed The Sharmanscopes on Phoenix Radio in Halifax as part of The Mike Sharman Show. They then continued to grow in popularity and he went on to publish them in written form in 2013, 2014 and 2020.

Mike is an author, lyricist, presenter and is currently preparing to star in pantomime.

Aged 44, Mike has three children and currently lives in the West Midlands, UK.

Mike can be found on social media using @mrmikesharman

Mike Sharman

FROM THE AUTHOR

I hope you enjoy my latest collection of comic predictions and that they bring a mix of laughter and groaning in equal measure, especially if you're sat next to somebody on the train when you're reading them!

A decade has passed since I first published a collection of Sharmanscopes and I continue to publish new material based on your overwhelming positive feedback and demand.

I sincerely thank you for this support and will continue the Sharmanscope journey for as long as the world seems to need them!

FROM THE PUBLIC

"They have the knack of correctly predicting my daily detours and disasters"

Alan Key

"I have a special place in my home for The Sharmanscopes - Under the wonky leg of my coffee table"

Godfrey Church

"They told me my lucky holiday destination was the Pyramids. He was right. I don't know how he Sphinx them up!"

Poppy Cox

"Hits all the right notes for me"

Amanda Lynn

And the genuine ones......

"Short and sweet groaners abound in The Sharmanscopes. Open season on all signs - great fun"

D Dobs (2013)

"Funny read - it's interesting to see what might happen to me in the future"

Floysh (2014)

"A genuinely funny book is one of life's simplest pleasures. Really recommend this, will make the perfect gift for someone who could do with cheering up"

Laura (2020)

THE SHARMANSCOPES IV (2023)

SUNDAY

AQUARIUS

Your day starts when you asked to give feedback on the new experimental car run on chip fat you received last week. You report to the garage that it does 350 miles to the gallon and lets off very few fumes. However, you did have to stop every 25 miles to change the vinegar.

Your uncle, who was a poet, is finally buried today and is taken to the crematorium in a car covered in the words of his best poems. Well, he did always want to go out in a verse.

You are sad to hear about another raft of job losses at the local scissors making factory today, but you hope these will be the final cuts.

Lucky Chocolate Flavour: Salted Caramel

Lucky Simpsons Character: Krusty The Clown

PISCES

You read an article today which reveals that an Irishman has successfully consumed 36 pints of stout in a row. He has made it into the World Record Book of Guinnesses.

You cause confusion at the doctor's surgery today when the doctor looks in your mouth and says to you "a little roar". You answer "rawwwr!"

You accept an invitation to join the virtual get-together meeting of the UK Rat Catchers Society today, deciding it is a good thing for you all to swap tails.

Lucky Fish: Rainbow Trout

Lucky Mobile Phone App: Candy Crush

ARIES

Your wife reveals to you today that she was born in a field surrounded by apple trees. You think this is why you find her so appealing.

You cause an argument on your online Classics course today when you ask if Roman doctors and paramedics referred to IVs as 4s?

An attempted romantic gesture backfires today as you listen to the hints from your wife to take her to a Spa. Sadly, the type that sells pasties and newspapers isn't quite what she had in mind.

Lucky Hashtag: #bigdipper

Lucky Telephone Directory Page Number: 113

TAURUS

You are excited to hear that your neighbour has been selected for the Gardening Olympics today. Having watched him in action, you have high hopes that he will secure a medal in the fencing event.

You not only fall out with your local farmer but are also chased off his land today when you say to him "Isn't it amazing how the holes in a cat's fur are in just the right spot for its eyes?"

A long discussion about what to eat for dinner tonight results in your wife saying to you "I want you to make me chilli". So you carry her outside and lock the doors.

Lucky Candle Scent: Vanilla

Lucky Power Tool: Chainsaw

GEMINI

You witness a car crash today and try to help. You notice an injured passenger on the pavement and try to assure him that a Red Cross nurse is on the way. The injured man complains, "Can't I have a cheerful blonde one instead?".

Problems on the dating front are likely when you invite your girlfriend for a seven course meal. It turns out that a pizza and a six pack is not what she had in mind.

You continue to encounter problems with your new job helping to look after cars at the local motor racing track today. Your friends think the job sounds great but you tell them that it's the pits.

Lucky Stamp: 2nd Class Stamp

Lucky Seafood: Crab

CANCER

You recall a trip to the rainforest today. Your local guide was checking for buffalo herds. He put his ear to the ground and said "Ugg. Deer come". Amazed, you asked him how he knows that. "Easy", he said "Ear sticky".

After a month of sticking with it, you decide your abandon your road cycling ambitions today as you find it keeps making you two-tired.

You end the day in amazement at the accuracy of an online palm-reader's revelations about your past. You really have to hand it to her.

Lucky Colour: Brown

Lucky Christmas Decoration: Tinsel

LEO

You watch a TV programme tonight which claims that smut is the very last thing you will find on the show. They are correct. You have to wait 56 minutes for it.

You visit a local church today and are amazed at the strength of the two church wardens who spent over an hour carrying heavy books from one part of the church to another. You put it down to the strength in their psalms.

You are angered to find that boxers are reportedly going to be first to get a new Flu vaccine next week. They always seem to be first to the jab.

Lucky Fruit: Watermelon

Lucky Monopoly Square: Bond Street

VIRGO

Your snooker-playing best friend loses in the qualifying round of a major tournament again today without scoring a single point. This is the fifth time since his marriage collapsed and his house subsided. You wonder when he is going to get a break in life.

Your plans for a radical reality TV show reboot are rejected today when TV bosses reveal that dressing contestants as a singing Jesus for the programme "Pop Idol" is not what they have in mind.

You try to help your child with a costume for World Book Day today. Remembering mini books you got in cereal packets years ago, you dress your son up as Kellogg's Tony The Tiger. However, this leads to a frosty reception despite you insisting he looks grrrrrrrreat.

Lucky Technical Item: Amazon Echo

Lucky Body Part: Big Toe

LIBRA

Your jungle expedition is interrupted today when two lions start having sex in front of your safari jeep. "Have they no pride?" you complain to the driver.

Your ongoing battle with the farming community continues today when you speak to a farmer on your daily walk and he tells you that his farm is arable. You reply "Why, what's wrong with it?"

You buy a miniature Japanese radio today for when you next go on holiday. You intend to put it in your swimming trunks when you are on the beach. It may look odd but gets you a great reception.

Lucky Man's Name: Trevor

Lucky Takeaway Dish: Sweet and Sour Chicken

SCORPIO

You hit success in the garden today when your crossing of a marijuana plant with a fruit tree starts producing plums which are already stoned.

Problems are likely on the entertainment front today, specifically with your television. The arrival of agonising hernia pain means that you cannot pick anything up.

The day ends with you getting the silent treatment from your wife when you suggest to her that your love life is like an electrical plug. You say that you are live, she is neutral and you can't make the earth move.

Lucky Fizzy Drink Flavour: Orange

Lucky Radio Station: BBC Radio One

SAGITTARIUS

Your efforts in the kitchen do not go down well today. Whilst sat at the dinner table you tell your wife that you made this meal from scratch. She replies "well you should send it to a dermatologist then".

You finally receive news of which emergency service you are being placed with today. It is Search and Rescue. You are happy to hear this as you feel you have a real flare for it.

The day ends with an argument when you and your wife discuss the old entertainers The Tiller Girls. You tell your wife that she looks like a tiller. Atilla The Hun.

Lucky Train Carriage: C

Lucky Thermostat Temperature: 19 Degrees

CAPRICORN

You receive a Zoom call from your neice today who tells you that she has set up her own knitwear company which is doing very well and she starts to show you her jumpers.

You are unsure if she is telling the truth or if she is pulling your eyes over her wool,

You are pleased to hear news today that a pocket watch is to be named after you. It saddens you however to read the desciption which says "it ticks ok, but tocks too much".

The day ends in confusion as you sit down to watch a horror film called "Don't Open The Door" only to discover that it is all about Jehova's Witnesses.

Lucky Pudding: Treacle Sponge

Lucky Fence: Becher's Brook

MONDAY

AQUARIUS

Your day starts in comedy fashion as you read a story about a hapless miserable Australian man. It turns out that his boomerang left him but his wife kept coming back.

The comedy continues when you receive a party invite to an exclusive party event at a friend's house. You presume a typo has been made as the invite reads "Wife and Cheese Tasting Party".

You end the day reading a news article revealing that genes are responsible for people having crossed-eyes. You think is especially true if the jeans are tight.

Lucky Garden Bird: Blackbird

Lucky Scrabble Word: Brouhaha

PISCES

You read today that in Iran, if you commit aldultery then you get stoned. You think this is unusual as in the UK, you suspect it is the other way around.

You try to enter an online competition today but struggle with a question asking you to name all of the actors who have ridden in the Tardis as the Doctor. You later find the answer in "Who's Who".

A memo from the bank at which you work reveals plans to wash all of the money it handles to remove all germs which may be present. You suspect this is a form of money laundering.

Lucky Novellist: Jeffrey Archer

Lucky Ice Lolly: Twister

ARIES

You encounter problems today when you are timed out of your weekly online quiz when you attempt to answer the question "What is another name for a thesaurus?".

You are encouraged at your amateur dramatic rehearsal at a local theatre today when the producer says to you "get out there, where you belong". Your happiness turns sour when you notice he is pointing at the exit.

The day ends with you considering taking up computer dating. After some thought, you decide they would be too awkward to cuddle and have too much internal memory.

Lucky Item Price: 65 Pence

Lucky Footwear Item: Wellington Boot

TAURUS

The day starts in odd fashion today when your visit your local bank and say to the Bank Manager, "How do I stand for a £25,000 loan?". He replies by suggested you drop to your knees and pray.

Later you meet up with an attractive female friend of yours who works as a dental assistant. Wanting to impress her, you order her a drink; a pair of teeth.

You end the day watching a programme on TV all about a man who claims to own a singing dog. When it comes to the moment for the dog to prove it can sing, all it can do is Bach.

Lucky Quiz Round: Music

Lucky Photo Size: 8 x 10 Inches

GEMINI

Your try to enter your dog into a competition today but when you asked what breed of dog it is, you answer "allsorts". You later discover it has been entered into the Basset category.

You make a scientific discovery today that sound cannot travel through a perfect vacuum. This is why you never heard your pet cat in the hoover.

You work on your extended family tree this evening and find that your great-great-grandfather was taken prisoner at Waterloo. They found him trying to steal some luggage.

Lucky Country: Italy

Lucky Sporting Item: Shuttlecock

CANCER

You find yourself staggering home drunk today and walk past a man working on his car. "What's the problem?" you ask the man, who replies "Oh, piston broke". You then reply "Yeah, me too".

A similar problem hits your work life today as you are sacked as a teacher having been found making love to the least attractive single female teacher at school. Gross Miss Conduct.

You go to watch a women's ice hockey game tonight and can't believe how long the game goes on for. Then you realise why. They have to change their pads after every period.

Lucky Football Score: 3-2

Lucky Sunday Roast Item: Apple Sauce

LEO

The days starts on frosty ground when your wife suggests you call one another by a pet name. You decide to call her Shergar as you hope she disappears.

Things get little better as you visit the doctor's surgery. As you walk into the consulting room, the brand new doctor says to you, "You have an iron deficiency". Amazed you ask her how she can possibly know that as you have just walked in. She answers "Your shirt is creased".

The day ends with you watching the news to discover that one of your neighbours has been arrested for stealing sweets from the factory she worked at by smuggling them out in her underwear. Police are referring to her as Smartie-Pants.

Lucky Text Abbreviation: BRB

Lucky Hotel Star Rating: Three Star

VIRGO

You find yourself tested in a flight simulator today and only just manage to land the plane inches short of an accident. You say to this instructor "That's the shortest runway I've ever seen". She looks sideways and says "Yes, but it's the widest".

You bump into your ex-wife today who asks how thigs are. You say good and that you are really enjoying microwave meals. She seems unsurprised, saying "You always liked satisfying your urges in under three minutes".

You sister calls you today to update you on the new job she started last week in a paperless office. She tells you it is going well but going to the toilet is challenging.

Lucky Shape: Circle

Lucky Washing Machine Setting: Quick Wash

LIBRA

You hear news break this morning of a terrible accident at Spaghetti Junction. Over ten people are injured and three pasta way.

You annoy a local zoo worker today when you ask him what you call an aardvark that's just been beaten up? After he tells you he doesn't know, you answer "A vark".

The days ends with you giving blood. It may not be the traditional gift to give to your wife on your anniversary, but at least it came from the heart.

Lucky Salutation: Reverend

Lucky Toolbox Item: Stanley Knife

SCORPIO

Online shopping goes wrong for you today when your try to order digital platform shoes. Sadly when they arrive they are not a true pair. One is Facebook whilst the other is Twitter.

You fall out with a French friend of yours today on a Zoom call. You ask him, "What do you get when you toss a hang grenade into a kitchen in France?". As he doesn't answer, you say, "Linoleum Blownapart".

You cheer yourself by watching an online performance from a man who performs magic using chocolate. He has a lot of Twix up his sleeves.

Lucky Alcoholic Drink: Lager and Lime

Lucky Pet: Parrot

SAGITTARIUS

You annoy the local firefighters today when you see them leaving the station at the end of their shift, all wearing casual clothes. You shout and say they should be wearing blazers or smoking jackets.

You try to get some advice from your best friend today about a problem that's been worrying you. You ask him if his penis burns after sex. "I don't know", he says "I've never tried to light it".

You discover today that your Auntie, who is an accomplished artist, has started touring the UK in a van to showcase her art. She is calling herself Winnie Bay Gogh.

Lucky Actor: Rowan Atkinson

Lucky Female Name: Jennifer

CAPRICORN

You are pleased to receive a Dyson Ball Cleaner today as a gift. Caution is advised however, as misunderstanding what it is used for could result in a trip to A&E.

You fall out with your local female vicar today when you ask if the reason God created Adam before he created Eve was that he didn't want anybody telling him how to make Adam.

You end the day returning from the doctor's and you tell your wife that your doctor thinks you are paranoid. You tell her that he didn't say this, but you are sure he's thinking it.

Lucky Sandwich Filling: Chicken & Stuffing

Lucky Body Part: Nipple

TUESDAY

AQUARIUS

You catch up via video call with a friend of yours today who is a vet. She tells you that she recently bought a book called "The Immortal Dog" and since then she hasn't been able to put it down.

You are invited to a Wild West themed party today and go dressed in a cowboy costume made out of tin foil. You are soon asked to leave however as they become worried about your rustling.

Confusion in the bedroom ends the day when you and your partner are cuddling in bed and she asks you if you have got any fantasies. You reply, "I've got a couple of Terry Pratchett books".

Lucky Christmas Cracker Item: Paper Hat

Lucky Finger: Middle Finger

PISCES

Your excitement at the arrival of your new metal detector is dampened today when you take it out into your garden to use and dig a 45 foot hole before you realise you are wearing steel toe-cap boots.

More fortunate happenings are predicted when you open a letter telling you that you have won the local joke competition. Your entry was "What do you call a man with a spade in his head? An ambulance".

The day ends with an unfortunate mix up as you pick up and wear your wife's glasses by mistake. This results in you knocking things over and walking into a door in front of your children. You vow to never make a spectacle of yourself again.

Lucky Tennis Shot: Backhand

Lucky True Or False Answer: True

ARIES

You cause confusion at a restaurant today. You decide to order chicken soup, but as the waiter is walking away change your mind on the flavour. You shout to the server "Hold the chicken, make it pea".

You visit your doctor later in the day but are concerned that he is getting things wrong as he asks you to hold him as he coughs.

You end the day in disagreement with your wife when she tells you that she wants to buy the latest cleaning products advertised on television. You insist that you wait for a year when they will then be "new and improved".

Lucky Vegetable: Carrot

Lucky Snooker Ball Colour: Blue

TAURUS

You start the day with joy which quickly turns to disappointment. The joy starts when you receive a letter informing you that you have won an award for your new book about prostitutes. Despair kicks in when you re-read the letter and the award is called "The Hooker Prize".

You read an article in the newspaper today about a new TV programme where criminal cases are heard by dogs. It is to be called "Woof Justice".

You end the end deciding to write another book. This time it will be all about ways to make day-to-day taskes easier using drawing pins. You decide to call it "A collection of daily life tacks".

Lucky Olympics Event: Pole Vault

Lucky Telephone Dialling Code: 0141

GEMINI

You decide it is time to lose weight today having visited the opera for a performance last night and nobody would let you leave before you had sung a song.

You speak with some surgeon friends of yours today and ask them what they do with old medical equipment when it is ready to be replaced. They tell you they put it all in an old emergency operation room. When you ask why, they say "it's useless for all intensive purposes".

You end the afternoon in argument with your chemist who insists that the cream he has given you to enlarge your manhood should be applied by hand twice a day. You argue that if it works, wouldn't your hand size double within a few days?

Lucky Room Scent: Lavender

Lucky Nursery Rhyme Character: Little Miss Muffet

CANCER

You discuss your odd behaviour around cheese with a neighbour today. You tell her that you can't eat cheese on sandwiches, toast, cocktail sticks or anthing like that: only on little biscuits. She quickly decides that your behaviour is crackers.

Your doctor suggests to you today that you need to give up 50% of your sex life due to your increasing age. So you ask her which half, the thinking about it or the talking about it?

You cause upset trying to help at a local ex-servicemen's delayed Christmas party today. You dress a veteran up in tinsel, baubels and flashing lights. This is not what was meant by a "decorated hero".

Lucky Tarot Card: The Hermit

Lucky Ale: Ruby Stout

LEO

You find yourself being cast as King Kong in an amateur production today but are quickly told that you need to purchase 15 pairs of shoes. When you question why, you are told that he was a 30 foot monster.

You spend a chunk of today worrying endlessly about New Year's Eve later this year. After a while, you put it down to Auld Langxiety.

The days ends with you learnind that the army plan to employ new weapons made from potatoes. Despite assurances, you are unsure that spud missiles and weapons of mash destruction will be effective.

Lucky Cathedral: Coventry Cathedral

Lucky Egg: Hard Boiled

VIRGO

You fall out with your local vicar today when you ask him if the link between chromosomes and the Bible is that XY is Adam, XX is Eve and YYY Delilah.

You are disappointed today when you go the cinema to watch "Thor" and discover that it is not the sequel to "Frozen".

You decide to write a book of poems today until a friend convinces you to write longer in-depth stories instead. You think that this is a novel idea.

Lucky Car Gear: Third

Lucky Socks Colour: Blue

LIBRA

Your wife queries your thinking this morning as you strip naked in front of the mirror, look at yourself and say "Should I diet?. Before you wife can answer, you add "and if so, which colour?".

You enter into an interesting discussion in your local bank today when withdrawing money. The cashier says "All in legal tender". You ask why she says "tender" and she answers "because if you haven't got any money it's tough"!

The day ends with an upsetting letter from your child's school for which you fully get the blame. It turns out your son answered the Teacher's question, "What is a pocket calculator?" with "The name my Dad gives to my Mom when she goes through his pockets at home".

Lucky TV Remote Button: Mute

Lucky Cooking Sauce: Bechamel

SCORPIO

Your day starts with an unfortunate misunderstanfing today when you follow a recipe which says "chill in the fridge for an hour". After half an hour, you decide it is too cold and cramped for you.

You raise a chuckle later in the day when a comedian suggests on TV that Charles Ingram is to appeal the decision to withold the £1million he "won" on "Who Wants To Be A Millionaire". He is claiming that his wife and Tecwen Whittock had Covid.

You end the day reading a science journal which reveals that pornography is giving young people an unrealistic and unhealthy idea of how quickly a plumber will come to your house.

Lucky Sandwich Filling: Crab Paste

Lucky Military Rank: Captain

SAGITTARIUS

You become concerned today that your decision to go the local gym religiously has meant you looked a fool running on the treadmill dressed as a vicar.

You find yourself being fired today as a government virus advisor. When you ask them why you have been sacked, they tell you that you didn't know your SARS from your Ebola.

You end the end finalising a plan to steal low calorie yoghurts from your local supermarket. It really is taking shape.

Lucky Biblical Figure: Noah

Lucky Horse Riding Item: Whip

CAPRICORN

You enter a joke competition today and try to tell a joke about shops not accepting money and only taking card payments but you cannot think of one ATM.

Marital arguments maybe predicted today when you comment to wife that women's golf is very lifelike - they are poor drivers but great with an iron.

You decide to try and cash in on the Covid crisis tonight by selling vaccines. You plan to offer a vaccine for £2 or 3 for a Pfizer.

Lucky Pie: Chicken & Mushroom Pie

Lucky Dance: The Conga

WEDNESDAY

AQUARIUS

News breaks this morning that the latest goal-line technology is finally ready to be launched in Scotland. Hawk Eye, The New.

Problems with the wife are likely today when you read that if you can taste paper or cardboard, you may have Covid. So you apologise to your wife for criticising her cooking, saying you've had Covid for over 20 years.

As a former maths teacher, you decide to take on a temporary job as a Greggs delivery driver today. You tell them that you can only deliver to Hull, Grimsby and Scunthorpe. When asked why, you answer that you were trained to only take pie to three dismal places.

Lucky Newspaper Page: 17

Lucky TV Actor: David Jason

PISCES

With news of a possible crisis today, you notice a man buying four cases of San Miguel, three paellas and six sombreros. You think to yourself Hispanic Buying.

Disappointment is expected today when the carpenter you had paid to make you a double bed decides to do a bunk.

You end the day turning your sofa into a sofa bed. You do this instantly by forgetting it is your wife's birthday.

Lucky Car Part: Hubcap

Lucky Garden Item: Birdbath

ARIES

Your day starts with the late arrival of your online cosmetics order which you placed some months ago. You decide not to complain about the delay as it's better late than Nivea.

Your ongoing battle with the farming community reignites today when you call a radio phone-in on cattle farming in Yorkshire to ask if all the cows live in Uddersfield. Your decision to repeat the joke for heffer and heffer does not go down well.

The day ends with a trip to hospital when you child accidentally eats a guitar and ends up with strummock trouble. The doctors tell you not to fret and you appear to be highly strung.

Lucky Quiz Category: Science & Nature

Lucky Museum: The Black Country Living Museum

TAURUS

You find yourself in a mistaken-identity incident today, which sees you being arrested for shoplifting from your local supermarket. The real culprit was later found to be hiding in the gravy store room, where he was taking stock.

You are pleased to finally be able to taste your home-brewed carrot wine today. You find that it still makes you drunk but you are able to see better.

You decide to upgrade your supermarket today from Aldi to Waitrose. You notice a number of differences, the main one being that the fish fingers are now manicured.

Lucky Crayon Colour: Yellow

Lucky Sauce: Tartare Sauce

GEMINI

You cause confusion at the local library today when you ask for "one of those thinner books about hospital operations". The Librarian doesn't understand what you mean so you add "The ones with the appendix removed".

You annoy your local MP today when you met him whilst out walking. You tell him that you are not going to vote again because whoever ends up in Number 10, we will still be in Number 2.

You win a competition today where you had to name two Charles Dickens novels to be featured on a new banknote. You suggested "Great Expectations" for when times are good and "Hard Times" for when they are not!

Lucky Hotel Room Number: 215

Lucky Cheese: Feta

CANCER

Your day starts in unusual style at work when your boss asks you if you could do your job in your sleep? You answer, "Yes", and she replies "Well do it then because you mess it up when you're awake".

A bout of stomach pain sees you needing to visit the hospital today. You insist on taking a red crayon with you in case you need to draw blood.

Later in the day, you decide to take up fencing but the Police insist you have to put it back it back tomorrow.

Lucky Charity Shop: Oxfam

LEO

You make friends with a Frenchman on a Zoom call today and you ask him if he likes video games. He answers "Wii".

Sticking with technology, you visit a computer repair shop today and ask why your iPad is making you sleepy. They tell you that there's a nap for that.

You enter a stand up comedy competition tonight and tell jokes which are all about coronavirus. Unfortunately the audience has to wait two weeks to see if they get it.

Lucky Boxing Weight: Featherweight

Lucky Scrabble Word: Quiz

VIRGO

You mistake two online exams today, one for Shakespeare's Romeo and Juliet and one for medicine. You fail the first with coronavirus and the second with a Verona crisis.

Somebody tries to attack you with a novel and a collection of poetry today. You rush to inform the Police and tell them everything, chapter and verse.

You end the day considering whether a child born during the last Lockdown will be a Quaranteen in the year 2033.

Lucky Toilet Part: Seat

Lucky Olympic Event: High Jump

LIBRA

You start today trying to kick start your career as a stand-up comedian telling jokes about cricket. Sadly it doesn't work. Your jokes are good but your delivery is poor.

You find yourself in hot water at your local Post Office today when you ask the Post Mistress, "If the world is getting smaller, why do the prices of stamps keep going up?".

Your day ends in worrying fashion when, on an unplanned night out, you open a fortune cookie which contains a note from your wife telling you to come home at once.

Lucky Tinned Food: Baked Beans & Sausages

Lucky Breakfast Item: Coco-Pops

SCORPIO

Your day starts angrily when you read about a case of combine harvester killings in the newspaper where the suspects were baled.

You manage to fall out with your blonde female neighbour today when she tells you she has adopted a zebra at the zoo. You laugh loudly when she tells you she has called it spot.

You then manage to fall out with your elderly quiz team friends when you answer the question "What's the best form of birth control after 50?" with "Nudity".

Lucky Candle Scent: Vanilla

Lucky Cluedo Suspect: Professor Plum

SAGITTARIUS

You day starts badly when your wife says to you she thinks she is putting on weight and you tell her to go to the DIY store as she can get thinner there.

Disaster with the car is predicted today when you back the car out the garage before remembering you backed it in the night before.

You end the day disovering that Robinson Crusoe invented the 40 hour working week. He had it all done by Friday.

Lucky Elevator Button : Alarm

Lucky Wrestler : The Undertaker

CAPRICORN

You visit the doctor today and ask him "Look Doc, just tell me, how do I stand?". He replies "I don't know. It's a miracle".

You cause annoyance in an electrical shop today by asking for someone crazy about electricity. The store manager asks you what you mean and you tell her that you want an electric fan.

You fall out with the local vet today by asking him if you should call a septic cat "Pus".

Lucky Hospital Department : Maternity

Lucky Airline : Easyjet

THURSDAY

AQUARIUS

Your doctor asks you today if you drink to excess. You tell him that you drink to anything.

You cause uproar in the musical pet shop today by answering the question "Is anything worse than spiders on your piano?" with "Yes. Crabs on your organ".

You try to tell the time by looking at the sun today, but fail as you can't see the numbers.

Lucky Gardening Tool : Trowel

Lucky Cheese : Stilton

PISCES

You decide to take up tarot readings today, having determined success in on the cards.

You question your choice of pet dog today when you accidentally cut your hand and your bloodhound fainted.

You are stunned by your child tonight when you question them about not having the highest marks in class. They answer "Do you have the highest salary in your office?".

Lucky Island : Isle of Wight

Lucky Hymn : All Things Bright And Beautiful

ARIES

You quit your job as a historian today having decided there is no future in it.

A chef friend of yours causes confusion today by naming his pet horse "Radish". He does this so he can say "Here's my horse Radish".

Health problems are predicted today as you kiss a canary and come down with chirpes. You then decide to tweet about it.

Lucky Book Chapter : 7

Lucky Street Name : Park Road

TAURUS

Success is predicted in a joke competition today when you enter with "Charles Dickens goes into a bar and orders a Martini. The barman says Olive or twist?".

Animal problems may occur today when your dog makes sexual advances towards a cabbage. The dog thinks it is a collie.

You later decide to rename your dog as he can find absolutely anything. You call him Labragoogle.

Lucky Spirit : Drambuie

Lucky Superhero : Bananaman

GEMINI

Your 15 year quest to find a cure for bad breath and baldness ends disappointingly today when you realise that people don't like you anyway.

You read in the newspaper today that an amputee robber evaded police capture for three weeks. You think this was amazing considering he wasn't armed.

Your career as an airline pilot is under scrutiny today when Air Traffic Control ask for your height and you reply "Six foot".

Lucky Hotel Room Item : Hair Dryer

Lucky Petrol Pump Number : 3

CANCER

You awaken this morning to your partner pouring petrol over you in bed. You report this to police who ask you

"What do you think she was going to do to you?". You reply "I'm not too sure but think she was trying to make a fuel of me".

You cause an accident of your own later by falling asleep at the wheel. Clay goes absolutely everywhere.

You end the day at a car boot sale and buy some Harry Potter games. They're a quid each.

Lucky Musical : Fame

Lucky TV Chef : Gordon Ramsey

LEO

Your close friend loses their job as a theatre designer today. You are just glad that he left without making a scene.

You are rejected at the application stage for Dragon's Den today. It turns out that Tampax with bells and tinsel for the Christmas period is not an acceptable idea.

You chat with elderly neighbour today who tells you he feels like a newborn baby. No hair, no teeth and he's just wet his pants.

Lucky Computer Game : Jet Set Willy

Lucky Karaoke Song : Waterloo

VIRGO

A misunderstanding causes damage and near-death today when you install a new smoke alarm on your lounge ceiling. You then notice it says "test your alarm is working properly" before setting fire to your sofa.

Your family tree research comes up trumps today when you find that your grandfather had his tongue cut out in the war. You realise this must be why he doesn't talk about it.

You end the day renewing your arguments with local religious groups by asking a Jehovah's Witness if, when they die and go to Heaven, God hides behind the gates and pretends he's not in?

Lucky Washing Cycle : Spin

Lucky Bakery Store Item : Iced Bun

LIBRA

You notice an old advert for Marks & Spencer today which says that it wouldn't be Christmas without M&S. You realise they are right. It would be Chrita.

You once again cause argument in your pub quiz tonight by answering "What's soft and warm when you go bed but hard and stiff when you wake up?" with "Vomit".

You also find yourself in serious trouble today for urinating in the shower. Despite your defence, this is not acceptable on the shopfloor in B&Q.

Lucky Surname : Lilley

Lucky Dartboard Segment : Double Nine

SCORPIO

You start the day reading sad news about the death of anti-road protestor. He refused a bypass.

You attend a sex convention today but are asked to leave when you ask if an atheist yells "Darwin, Oh Darwin" when enjoying an orgasm.

You are also thrown out of a local allotment today when you ask a gardner what he calls his two rows of cabbages. Before he can answer you say "A dual cabbage-way".

Lucky Pub Quiz Subject : Sport

Lucky Boxing Weight : Heavyweight

SAGITTARIUS

You receive sad news today that a close friend of yours has drowned in a half-empty bath tub. You think to yourself this is such a shame as he was so optimistic.

You walk past a kitchen furniture shop today and notice a sign in the window saying "Stainless steel sinks". You think to yourself that this is a bit obvious before walking on.

The day ends with you being attacked in the local park by a couple of youths with bats. Despite the attck, you can't help but be impressed with how well they had trained them.

Lucky TV Channel : BBC News

Lucky Vegetable : Cucumber

CAPRICORN

Your application to join a dating group is rejected today when you answer "What do call somebody who expects sex on the second date?" with "Patient".

You may enjoy success in a joke competiton today with the entry "What do you call the coolest person at the hospital? The Ultra-Sound Guy!"

You day ends in annoyance when you try to get advice by calling the Incontinence hotline, but they ask if you can hold.

Lucky Pet Name : Timmy

Lucky Vitamin : Vitamin B

FRIDAY

AQUARIUS

You pull in your stomach when weighing yourself today which sees you being told off by your wife. "That won't help" she says. You tell her "Of course it does, it's the only way I can see the numbers".

You fall out with a delivery driver today when he knocks on your door with a parcel for your next door neighbour. You tell him he has the wrong house then!

You end the day assaulting a laughing psychic and find yourself arrested for striking a happy medium.

Lucky Mixed Grill Item : Chicken Wing

Lucky McDonalds Dip : Sweet & Sour

PISCES

Problems in the park are predicted today when your picnic is interrupted by an old lady with a dog that keeps barking at you. You ask the owner if you can "throw her dog a bit". When she agrees, you pick the dog up and throw it into the pond.

You argue with doctor today when he tells you alcohol makes you fat and you insist it makes you lean.... against chairs, walls, doors...

Your visit to the doctor then continues with him asking you if you have a history of mental illness. When you answer "no", he gives you one.

Lucky European Country : Poland

Lucky Magazine : Elevator World

ARIES

You find yourself annoying your local hospital today when you arrive at A&E saying you have a case of Russian Measles. You say you have broken out in red squares.

You try to contend with your childhood memories today and realise you can't remember your parents ever asking somebody to pick you up when you were a child. You do however remember them asking a vet to put you down.

You end the day visiting a pub near a former house of yours. As you go in you say to the Landlady "It's been ten years since I came in here". She answers "Look, I'm doing my best, I'll be with you soon".

Lucky Starburst Flavour : Orange

Lucky Underwear Colour : Red

TAURUS

You try to convince a family member that your love of chocolate goes back to when your were 11 years old and first had a brownie today. They see through this however and the reason for you being kicked out of scouts is now clear.

You bump into a former girlfriend today who has recently toured Europe and you are surprised when she says to you that there's "nobody like you". Your pleasant reaction is then shattered when says "The French don't like you, the Italians don't like you .....".

You day ends with a chuckle when you contact a TV doctor. She diagnoses you, gives you one prescription and repeats all through the winter.

Lucky Mustard : Wholegrain Mustard

Lucky James Bond Film : Diamonds Are Forever

GEMINI

You may find yourself questioning your ability as a lover today when you realise you are being booed by a Peeping Tom.

The day gets no better when you visit your doctor to discuss your fear of heights. Sadly his response doesn't help when he says "Don't worry, in your career you won't be reaching any so nothing to worry about".

You visit a local airport today and ask about options to take up your interest in performing a skydive. However, when they say "Tandem?" to you, you leave deciding it would be too dangerous on a bike.

Lucky Supermarket Section : Cheese

Lucky Playing Card : Three of Hearts

CANCER

Your ability to annoy your Pub Quiz Team is evident again today when they ask you if you could hear someone call your name if you were in a vacuum and you answer "Is the vacuum on or off?".

You fall out with your well-educated girlfriend today when you tell her that having a girlfriend is a lot like applying to University. You rarely get an unconditional offer.

You end the day reading about an unusual case of a man who has been feeding gorillas with a golf club. He had been driving them bananas.

Lucky First Date Venue : Italian Restaurant

Lucky Tattoo Design : Rose

LEO

You remember today how your parents dropped you off at the wrong nursery on your first day at school. The photograph clearly shows you surrounded by trees and bushes.

Your read a story in the newspaper today about how a Simply Red fan has been arrested for having sex with an underaged rabbit. Apparently he was holding back the ears and the bunny was too tight to mention.

You lose your job at the Tickle Me Elmo production factory today when you are asked what is the last thing you do with them before they leave the factory? You answer, give them two test tickles

Lucky Over The Counter Medication : Optrex Eyedrops

Lucky Snack Item : Sausage Roll

VIRGO

You attend a 25-year school reunion today and realise that school must really have been a posh one. Even the gym is called James.

On the way back home from the pub today, you notice a drunken man shouting "Vodka" at passers-by. "That's the spirit" you think to yourself.

You reignite your battle with the local church today when you ask the Priest, "Why do Catholic women stop having children at 35?". You then answer "Because they think 36 is too many".

Lucky Brand of Cider : Thatchers

Lucky "Lucky Dip" Prize : Box of Crayons

LIBRA

Sad news starts your day today when your read that a major dog food company has gone bust and has had to call in the retrievers.

Bad news continues as you are told that your elderly neighbour has died at the shops from the big C. It's now known as "ostcutter".

The day ends with your relationship with a girl with a wooden leg in tatters when you decide to break it off.

Lucky Flapjack Ingredient : Sultanas

Lucky Communication Method : WhatsApp

SCORPIO

A potential new relationship turns sour on your online app today when your would-be suitor tells you she is a draftswoman. You tell her that your ex was the same; she never touched the bottled stuff.

You fall out with the local farmer later in the day when you ask him "Which side of a chicken has most feathers?" and then you quickly reply "The outside".

You end the day reading about a crime spree being led by a three fingered thief. He has being going around the city stealing ten-pin bowling balls.

Lucky Waste Collection Day : Wednesday

Lucky French Word : Jambon

SAGITTARIUS

You launch your new drink invention today a cross between Viagra and coffee called "Viagraccino". Early sales are likely to go well before people comment that after one cup they are up all night.

You find yourself in London today and realise that petrol prices must be really high. The Black Cab Drivers are taking the shortest route.

You once annoy annoy a local farm worker today who had been trying to show you how easy it is to milk a cow. Your reply of "so any jerk can do it" does not go down well.

Lucky Video Streaming Provider : Netflix

Lucky Car Part : Handbrake

CAPRICORN

You visit a cave today when a number of bats are hanging upside down from the roof. You then notice one bat stood upright on the floor concentrating straight ahead. You think to yourself it must be doing yoga.

You begin to think that you and your partner may have made a lot of loud noise during sex today as when you go into the back garden, even the neighbours are having a cigarette.

You then sit down to watch an episode of The Jeremy Kyle Show entitled "Can a man get a woman pregnant without physical contact?". You think to yourself, that's a long shot.

Lucky National Football Team : Wales

Lucky Thermostat Temperature : 16.5 Degrees

SATURDAY

AQUARIUS

You start the day trying to impress people with your job about lazy people but it just doesn't work.

Tragedy is on the cards today as your dog jumps into the washing machine before it started its cycle and died. At least it died in Comfort.

You cause uproar in your local shop today by asking for a loaf of bread. The shopkeeper sayd he has no bread but does have muffins. You ask him what is the difference. He answers "There's two f's in muffins and no f in bread".

Lucky Book Retailer: WH Smith

Lucky Credit Card : Barclaycard

PISCES

You experience some luck on the stock exchange today and manage to swap three oxo cubes for a jar of Bovril.

Your tells you this afternoon that when he goes to McDonalds, he always has a Happy Meal. You ask him why and he answers "I always leave my wife at home".

You find yourself chuckling at your brother's attempts to find love tonight as he places an advert on the noticeboard in the local pub saying "Wanted. Attractive landlady. Apply with inn".

Lucky Domino : Double Three

Lucky Swimming Stroke : Backstroke

ARIES

You start the day by hearing that a well-to-do friend's son has been expelled from a private school for taking cocaine. You think to yourself that he was born with a silver spoon up his nose.

You encounter difficulties checking into a hotel today when the receptionist asks you if you want a room with a shower or a bath. You ask him what's the difference and he answers "With a shower you have to stand up".

You end the day being thrown out of your science night school session. You were taking part in an experiment to prove that if you cut a worm in half, each half survives. Unfortunately you cut your worm lengthways.

Lucky Pasta Sauce : Carbonara

Lucky Stage Performer : Tommy Cooper

TAURUS

Your day starts badly at the doctors. You tell the doctor that you have an irrational fear that when you go to bed at night your young child will fall out of the cot and you won't hear it happen. You ask him what he thinks you should do and he tells you to pull up the carpet.

On your way back home you walk past the science college and find yourself chuckling at a sign on the back of a car there which reads "Particle physics gives me a hadron".

You go on a blind date tonight but are convinced you known the woman from somewhere. Then, during the lobster dish at the restaurant, you suddenly realise where you've seen thermidor.

Lucky Magic Trick : Dove Out Of A Hat

Lucky Number Of Calories In A Sandwich : 316

GEMINI

You are asked to leave a social event at a sports club today when a joke you tell goes badly wrong. The female manager did not appreciate "What's better than seeing a woman wrestle? Seeing her box".

Your TV appearance on the quiz show Countdown does not go to plan today. The nerves seem to get to you and you keep needing the toilet , leaving you feeling inconsonant and struggling to control your vowels. You think to yourself "What a conundrum".

You end the day drunkenly trying to walk on the buffet table at a birthday party. Your shouting of "I'm on a roll, this is a piece of a cake" does little to ease other guests anger.

Lucky Accompaniment To Cheese : Pickle

Lucky Spoon Size : Table Spoon

CANCER

You spend a chunk of today with solicitors as you discover you are being sued for your comedy act, specifically calling yourself "the complete jokebook". Somebody has complained because they found out you've had your appendix taken out.

You find yourself getting sacked from your job as a chef today as your boss realises you having been taking out of date lemons and limes home without telling him. You insist you've only taken the zest but he thinks you've been taking the pith.

You end the day winning a competition for a free month's use of the local sunbed / suntanning centre. You are unsure whether to be happy or browned off.

Lucky Classic Sweetshop Item : Strawberry Laces

Lucky Pie Filling : Steak & Ale

LEO

You annoy some Welsh friends of yours today when they invite you for a day with a Welsh harp. Unfortunately, you think this is an invite for a pint of lager in Swansea.

You start your job as a supermarket security guard today and quickly notice a young child crying who tells you she has lost her mother. You ask her "What's your mummy like?" and the little girl says "Smirnoff Ice and Pizza".

The days end with you in the dog house when your partner asks you to take them somewhere expensive. You both taje a trip to the petrol garage.

Lucky Nut : Pine Nut

Lucky Rose Colour : Pink

VIRGO

Your past history of crime comes in useful today when you join a dating website for arsonists. They send you new matches every day.

You spend some time watching the news today about war and you hear about a country fighting in a counter-offensive. You can't feeling that bullets may be more useful to them than counters.

Good news to end your day as your child receives their exam results from college. They do very well indeed and end up with more As than a Scouser trying to break up a fight.

Lucky Football Manufacturer : Mitre

Lucky Mobile Phone App : Weather

LIBRA

An expensive late night online purchase comes back to haunt you today. Last week you drunkenly ordered a penis enlarger for £95. Today it arrives and you are left feeling short-changed. It is a magnifying glass.

This afternoon, your wife tells you that she is fed with you pretending to be a flamingo. You have no option than to put your foot down.

You end the day excitedly visiting a local bookstore where you buy a copy of a new release entitled "37 mating positions". The book was already wrapped in brown paper for privacy so your first sight of it is at home. Disappointment soon kicks in when you open it and realise you have bought a book about chess.

Lucky Passport Page : 12

Lucky Letter In Alphabet Spaghetti : M

SCORPIO

You find yourself getting disqualified from a competition to find a new name for Viagra today. The judges were not impressed with "Mydixadrupin", "Dixafix" and "Ibepokin".

You visit a department store store with your friend who is a professional football team manager. He notices an elderly man struggling with his bags so goes over to him and asks "Can you manage Sir?". He replies "No. You got us into this mess, you'll have to get us out".

You end the day amazing a lady who had locked herself out of her car. You offer to help and take off your trousers before rubbing them against the car door to open it. Amazingly it works. You explain to her you have the same make of car so could use your khakis.

Lucky Weapon : Pea Shooter

Lucky Pub Name: The Kings Arms

SAGITTARIUS

You may cause some upset and confusion at a music festival today. You bump into a hippie and insist that his wife's name must be "Mississippi".

You watch an American sports programme on television today and notice a football coach yelling at a vending machine. You quickly realise that he wants his quarter back.

You may struggle with hayfever today which is no surprise as, when you go outside, you realise the pollen count is so high, even the bees are sneezing.

Lucky Comedy Show : Fawlty Towers

Lucky Fragrance : Brut

CAPRICORN

A prank backfires at the farm today when you sneak into the chicken house and replace all the eggs with brightly coloured ones. Things go wrong when the cockerel walks in, sees the eggs and rushes outside to beat up the peacock.

You think you have stumbled on a bargain today when you walk past a restaurant advertising chicken dinners for 50 pence. You order one, but when it arrives you get a plate full of bird seed.

The day ends with the Police knocking on your door to warn you about a cross-eyed burglar working in the area. They ask you that if you see him peering in your window, to warn the people next door.

Lucky Book : The Sharmanscopes

Lucky Tea : Mr T

Printed in Great Britain
by Amazon

23666989R00036